Intrusive Spills

J. Lenitiva

BookLeaf Publishing

India | USA | UK

Presentation by *BookLeaf Publishing*

Web: www.bookleafpub.com

E-mail: info@bookleafpub.com

ISBN: 9789358317770

First edition 2023

a child of a few words turned to be a woman of her own thoughts in her own world. the imagination runs rampant, it's hard to stay focused. but the dreams that scream are the stones that set. her fears are buried underneath her bruises. reconstruction is a lifetime process, so don't rush the masterpiece. keep a light in the fire and never burn out. take each as it's own and enjoy the different pieces of it. breathe. keep going. love. love. grow.

AUTHOR'S NOTE

Life is a beautiful thing, but life is hard, understood. But life is one and one, and you only get this one once. a story filled with nothin' but greatness, written by the best selling author. Can't lose, won't let it be an option. Gonna get what's coming and make sure it's the best. Remember, it's worth it.

PREFACE

breathe in.
breathe out.
it'll all be over soon.
release. relax.
the time will pass by soon.
five in. five out.
water will help it die soon.
sound on. sound up.
the waves will help the tension soon.

to the one leaving their
thoughts in a lock box:

a dream is never too dull
there aren't enough wishes in the wishing well
so let them burn brightly in the sky
a shooting star to wish for more shooting stars
something to look up to
while you wish for each day to be brighter

meditation.

The serine and brisk music,
giving off chill bumps that seem so surreal
The voice of the instruments harmonizing,
so soft spoken, yet such an impact.
The mind and soul whisked away
the body simply left breathless...
It's like Savasana on a floating cloud,
the flutes, the river water
the key elements

great man.

Have you ever had something that you never
wanted to let go of?
No matter how old you got,
What people would say or think,
You still kept it close.
Nothing can come in between,
You are what I keep close to me.
To love and appreciate for all my days.
You are the greatest thing to have
I found You and found peace.

dandelions.

i wish, i wish, upon a star,
life keeps me afloat
and takes me far.

to the moon and back,
to see the stars
to come back to earth and play my guitar.

paralyzed

Slipping back
is the worst thing possible
Melancholy Madness
not wanting to get up in the morning
not wanting to get up at all..
paralyzed in the mind, the body refuses to move
one day the sadness might break,
but for now,
the wait continues..

dear no one.

I love you past the moon and back
naming stars on the way to the next
I wish we could walk forever
maybe in the next lifetime
it won't hurt as much… 🖤

overload:

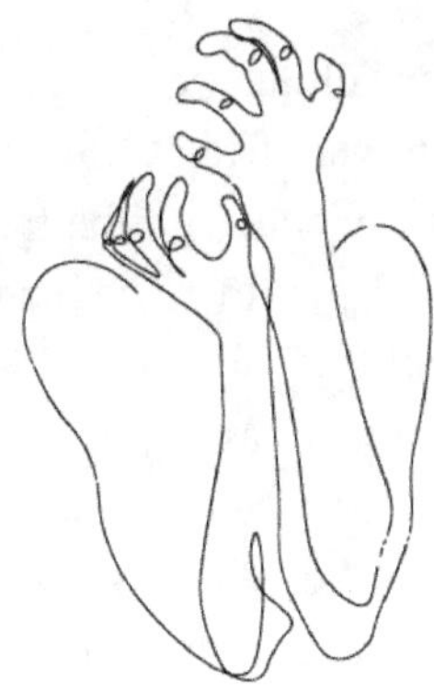

a million thoughts
yet none to write
The mind is so flustered
It begins to shut down

cheers.

Whewww chile..
if only it were friday,
i would say cheers to the freakin weekend.
but there's money to be made.
now don't get me wrong,
i don't mind chasing the money,
but why can't the money chase me?
you know, keep me on my toes.
give me a run for my money, that doesn't seem
to be enough.
as soon as i get it, i gotta give it right back,
ain't that some?
whewww, if only it were friday,
i can see it now cruisin to the music, wind
seducing my face wit it's soft touch and all.
Whew, just gotta make it a lil further.
i can't wait til it's friday,
i have so much to do this weekend,
things to do, places to be, people to see.
ahaaa it's friday, and i just got paid, do you
know what i mean.
Cheers to the freakin weeknd, baby.
the money has been made but them plans startin
to lookin a lil hazy as my eyes drag a lil bit..
Wheww chileee, thank God it's Friday,

i'm just gonna *yawn* yeaaa them plans can
miss me….
alarm rings
you're joking right…

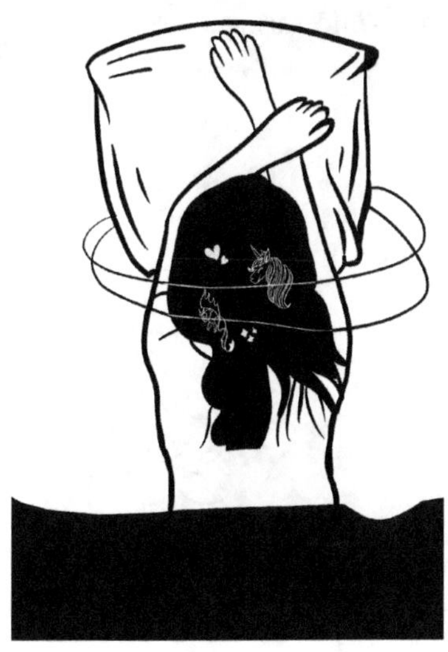

in bloom

bright as a sunflower, beautiful as a dozen roses
dark as the concrete it grew from
rooted in firm ground
though storms try to tear its delicacy
when the sun shines
simply bloom into form

distant lover

I am one of the most experienced inexperienced
lovers…
all the love in my body,
yet still haven't loved someone on the level I
desire.
yea, i know how love looks and how it's
returned platonically
but do I truly know what it takes to love?
i have a fantasy that there can only be one.
without truly having one in my catalog.
i dream of the high hopes that sweep the rug
from under me.
you can learn a person and what's underneath
without seeing what's underneath.
but it's like you see my hips spread and you
realize how much you want to spread me…
you dig in me deep without knowing you're
taking my soul.
well, maybe you do.
THE POINT IS, i want to be elevated,
not because of the works of my arch
but by the heights our minds can meet.
i don't want the fears of my inexperience to keep
me from experiencing what's out there.
but i feel like i'm in quicksand,

suffocating to tear from making this fantasy into reality.

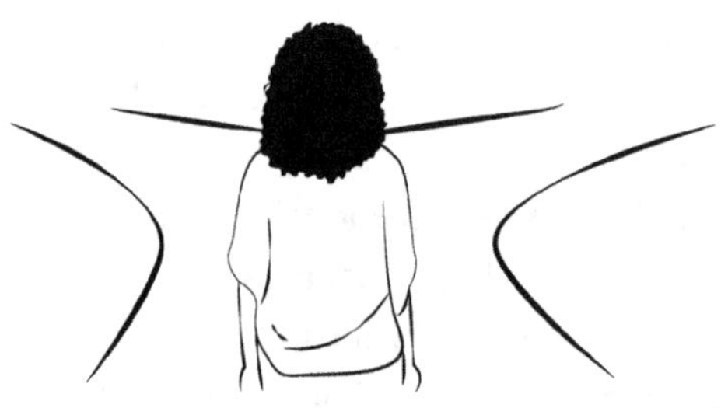

ungolden glitters.

in a world of perfection,
I want to be the one that completes you.
that missing piece for you
to make sure that even in darkness,
there's some light in your tunnel
I want to be the one you ease into after a long
day....
But we don't live in that world, do we?

stranger things

I'm new to love...
but I think about a lifetime with you

hate being around people...
but I want to sit with you and talk forever

I'm not the happiest person...
but I can feel my smile muscles showing when I
see you

Strange, right?

unknown:

I never was one to apply the force
but I always thought about it...
what happens beyond the red paint.

I was able to last another 40 seconds
I just hate you weren't able to come with me

♥

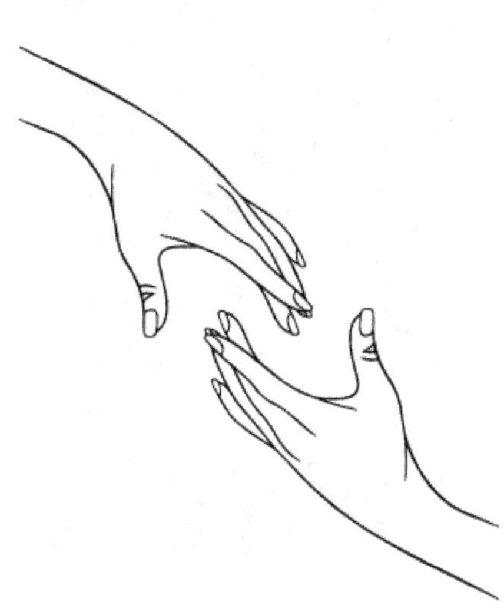

infinity and beyond

love beyond beauty
dead roses never lose their charm
dreaming of the deepest love
set this world on fire and desire
making all its memories
during volcanic eruption

meteor showers:

The night is on fire
so bright to match my eyes
starstruck of the damage it can do
mesmerized of it's beauty
I'm blinded
I don't wanna let go of that fire that burns.

synergy.

I close my eyes and imagine waves crashing the
sand
that mixed with raindrops can make the heart
flutter
the small breeze that grazes
hoping for the cue of thunder
but where the thunder rolls
the lightning sparks
so I just sit back
and wish for the spark of my trees
as I relax to the serine sounds.

tic tock

so quiet to hear a pen drop
even more to hear my heartbeat
I listen to drown the voices in my head
the mind that races
calming the amped beat
I sing to myself
breathe in. breathe out
so quiet to hear the wind whistle
too quiet to drift to sleep

Black Paint 🖤

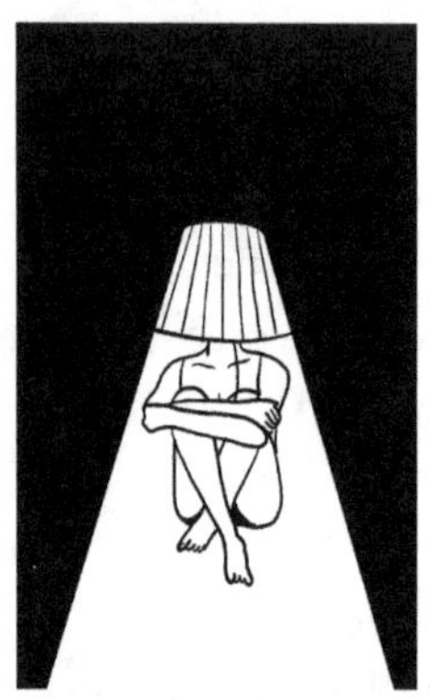

When I was a little girl,
I begged my parents to give me pretty black
paint on the walls of my room.
Pops simply said, "you not messin' wit my
walls"
Moms would only ask, "why would you want
such a dark color?"
I was too young to tell her the truth so I simply
kept quiet.
I thought she would feel some type of way
hearing her little girl tell her
I want my walls to comfort my fears of living,
Swallow the thoughts that bring me to tears
I need a color on my wall that can distract the
abstract graffiti made by my blood.
The darkness in my soul can fade into my lovely
black paint,

So that it wouldn't have to show on my face.
However, I am only a young girl
A small child who simply can't have a dark soul.
For it is believed to not be able to experienced at
a young age.
So I simply keep quiet, as I continue to keep my
white as clean as possible.

dive.

take a dive into the world.
to see the magic that lives within
the dreams and nightmares
they bring a sense of comfort.
or fear...
either way, it's a journey to remember.
know before you deal though,
play your cards right until the end.

note to self:

before starting this journey,
remember you are doing this not regarding
anyone's feelings but yours.
consider the response,
but do not stop your feelings from pouring out.
if something bothers you,
stop putting the bandaid over and let the truth
bleed.
one day there will be no more breath, let alone
feelings.
don't let it be too late to express your feelings.
bloom the way that makes you happy,
even if it makes everyone around uncomfortable.
even if it makes you uncomfortable...
pressure builds.
just don't blow.

The Prayer of Psalm 141

24

Lord, I am crying to you and I come to You
often,
I ask that You hear me.
Lifting my hands, Lord, is my way of giving my
all.
I come with all of my cares to You.
Please give me a door to guard my lips,
protecting what stays in and what goes out.
Keep my heart from anything or anyone that
shouldn't be.
When one is in a hard place, may they hear Your
voice.
You will not leave.
Keep away from the traps that are laid for me,
should I not fall to the low of others.

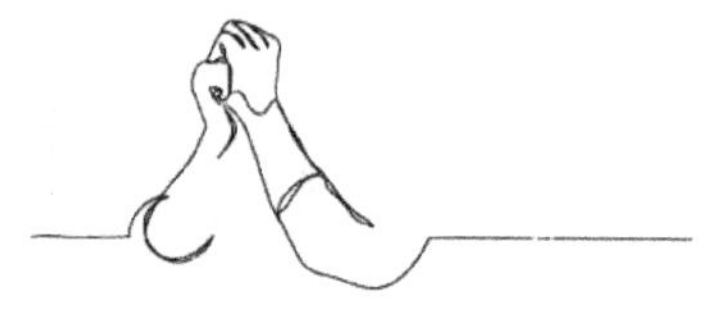